Thunder & Lightning

Andrea Rivera

abdopublishing.com

Printed in the United States of America, North Mankato, Minnesota
102016
012017

Cover Photo: Sme Beesley/Shutterstock Images
Interior Photos: Sme Beesley/Shutterstock Images, 1; Nikita Maykov/Shutterstock Images, 4–5; Clint Spencer/iStockphoto, 5; Sab Photo/Shutterstock Images, 6–7; iStockphoto, 9; Shutterstock Images, 10, 12, 13, 14–15, 15; Lisa Morrison/Herald & Review/AP Images, 11; Marc Simon Frei, 16–17; Dark Moon Pictures/Shutterstock Images, 18; Billion Photos/Shutterstock Images, 19; Dylan Haskin/Shutterstock Images, 21

Editor: Emily Temple
Series Designer: Madeline Berger
Art Direction: Dorothy Toth

Publisher's Cataloging-in-Publication Data
Names: Rivera, Andrea, author.
Title: Thunder & lightning / by Andrea Rivera.
Other titles: Thunder and lightning
Description: Minneapolis, MN : Abdo Zoom, 2017. | Series: In the sky |
Includes bibliographical references and index.
Identifiers: LCCN 2016948923 | ISBN 9781680799361 (lib. bdg.) |
ISBN 9781624025228 (ebook) | ISBN 9781624025785 (Read-to-me ebook)
Subjects: LCSH: Thunder--Juvenile literature. | Lightning--Juvenile literature.
Classification: DDC 551-dc23
LC record available at http://lccn.loc.gov/2016948923

Table of Contents

Science

Lightning is an electric spark.
It begins in a cloud.
It can go between clouds.
It can happen inside a cloud.

It can also travel from a cloud to the ground.

Air around lightning gets very hot. The air shakes. This makes a rumbling or cracking sound.

The sound is thunder.

Thunderstorms are the most common weather event on Earth. About 2,000 are happening at any moment.

Water and ice in **thunderclouds** bump into each other. They make **static electricity**. This causes lightning.

Computers show scientists where these clouds are.

Engineering

Lightning finds the easiest path to the ground.

So it seeks the nearest tall object.

Tall buildings often have **lightning rods**.

The rods send lightning safely to the ground.

Art

One artist makes photographs. They look like tiny thunderstorms. Wool becomes small clouds. **Tesla coils** shoot off sparks.

They look like lightning.

Math

Sound travels slower than light. So we hear thunder after we see lightning. Lightning might strike one mile (1.6 km) away.

We would hear thunder five seconds later.

- Lightning strikes the United States an average of 25 million times each year.
- The air around lightning gets up to 50,000°F (27,760°C). That is hotter than the surface of the sun!
- A town in Uganda gets the most thunderstorms of any place on Earth. It thunderstorms more than 240 days of the year there.

Glossary

lightning rod - a metal bar that attracts lightning so it doesn't strike and damage a building.

static electricity - energy produced by two objects rubbing together. It can create shocks or sparks.

Tesla coil - a device that produces bolts and sparks of electricity.

thundercloud - a huge, dark cloud that can cause hail, thunderstorms, or tornadoes.

Booklinks

For more information on thunder & lightning, please visit booklinks.abdopublishing.com

Zoom In on STEAM!

Learn even more with the Abdo Zoom STEAM database. Check out abdozoom.com for more information.

Index